Stand In Your POWER!

Alice Thompson

BookLeaf Publishing
India | USA | UK

Presentation by *BookLeaf Publishing*

Web: www.bookleafpub.com

E-mail: info@bookleafpub.com

ISBN: 9789357612142

First edition 2022

DEDICATION

This book is dedicated to the young girls that I teach today, that I have taught, and will teach in the future. To every single one of them, for showing up, working hard, laughing, crying, and being themselves in a world that wants them to all be the same. You are strong, you are beautiful, you are unique, you are powerful and you are YOU. There is no better person to be!

ACKNOWLEDGEMENT

I would like to take this opportunity to acknowledge some of the most wonderful people, who in many different forms, have helped me through some of the hardest times of my life, helped me see my worth and encouraged me to chase my dreams.

Thank you to Tina Mahon, Thomas Kelly, and Bert, who have encouraged me, supported me, celebrated with me and shown me that my words and voice matter.

Thank you to my beautiful friends Kirstie Taulbut, Joanne Hunt, Perdita Brown, O'desireé Hopkins, Tequila Gillespie, Jovan Watty, and Natasha Blackiston, who have always been solid and hilarious friends, I will forever be grateful.

A massive thank you to my Clubhouse family who have filled me with love and support from the very moment I spoke on stage, especially The Elliot and Jose Show and The A-game Consultancy Group, Adam[3] I am very grateful.

And last but not least, to my family, particularly my brother Gerard Thompson and sister Angela Thompson who have been my partners in crime, my rock, mischief masters and the hugs I needed when I forgot who I was.

PREFACE

In a world intent on creating carbon copies and unwritten oppression, women's voices are starting to be heard, but not enough and mainly through token politics. Women are still seen as objects of someone, or something and are expected to be grateful and thankful because for women in the UK, things are 'better' than they used to be. For some generations, it might be considered too late, but if my voice, through my poetry, helps just one woman or one girl discover their worth, then stepping out of my comfort zone and using my voice, through my written hand, has been worth it. As people, we do not get our worth through our education, our possessions or through being a mother, a sister, a daughter. We are human and that in itself is enough.

I have long hidden my love for poetry and spent most of my life believing I could never be a published poet. Well here it is - proof that you can step out of the box you are put in. This collection of poems explores what it is like to be a woman in a modern world that is still dominated by men. They explore losing and finding my voice and being an ally to all of my sisters and brothers. Speaking up about mental health, sexism, misogyny and the issues I see young women face. This doesn't mean men don't face them too. These poems are from my perspective, my view, my experience.

The roots of our actions and intentions speak higher volumes than our actions themselves. Stand In Your Power is a collection of poems, written in 21 days, with being open, honest and challenging myself as the root intention. I stand in my power - so you can safely stand in yours.

Stand in YOUR Power!

Stand in your power,
It is so unique.
It is drawn from you
And enthralled into me.

Stand in your power,
For those before you.
You are the example
Of bold, brave, and beautiful.

Stand in your power,
For it is so strong;
Defiant, fierce, brilliant.
It's where you belong!

Stand in your power,
You don't know who is watching.
Inspiring a generation
Of the long been lost,
Thinking they are nothing.

Stand in your power.
It was made for you,
Entirely and completely
By your evolving view.

Stand in your power.
Plant your feet.
Hold up your plaque.
March! Don't be discreet.

Stand in your power.
Reclaim it back.
Shout our song of equality.
It's time to change the track.

So stand in YOUR power,
For you are strong.
And stand in that power,
All day long!

Periodically Ignored

I was born a woman.
Biologically, that's what my body says,
And because of that burden,
Monthly my body experiences excruciating pain.

Doctors compare it
To the pain of labour,
Yet I'm expected to believe
That paracetamol and a hot water bottle
Are going to be my saviours.

Society's infrastructure
Doesn't want me to complain,
And each time my period comes
I'm expected to continue on my way.

I could be doubled over
Or in desperate need to change,
Popping tampons by the hour,
But it's just a period
The doctor explains.

They pump you with hormones
From the very first cycle.
Birth control for women
When they are only 6 days fertile.

No accountability for men,
The patriarchy has had its way.
"She must be on her period",
A misogynist's favourite phrase.

Money is poured into viagra research,
A lack of funding and care
For reproductive conditions,
Monthly leaving women in despair.

They want us to pretend it's not happening
And believe if we fight through - we will be
okay,
After all it's not an acceptable excuse,
A male controlled society in the modern day.

Our menstrual cycle controls us,
Our mind and body reacting differently
Day by day.
Society preaches kindness,
Self-care and to be mentally aware;
We all know the effects of a period.
The evidence has always been there.

Then why do we act
Like it isn't a thing?
Outwardly nothing is portrayed
Whilst inside of us a fire burns,

Tummies turn and minds wander away.
Hiding from the reality of what it truly is,
Our bodily systems left to cause us pain.

They won't give men the same drug,
But for women it's okay?!
We are left to struggle
And labelled unsanitary
When our period leaves us blood stained.

They wince at the mention of it
So we lock our products away.
Out of sight and out of mind,
A woman's silent fight,
As long as it is not in a man's way.
Pretending it isn't the part
Where life really starts…

But hey,

"It only lasts for a few days".

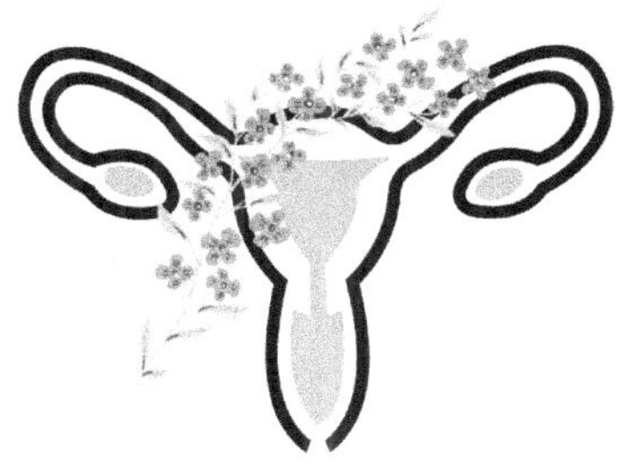

#SayHerName

It's in the news,
But it's not.
Another young woman's
Life lost.
Strictly dominates
The front pages.
Her name now lost
Amongst all the news stages.
The little article
Screams aloud
About how the woman
Was alone when out.
It was at night
In a public space.
In sight,
So why did it take
So long
For her to be traced?
Her picture shouts pride.
No more dodgy photos
From a fun night.
In her robes of success,
To show the world
She wasn't the problem -
It was men!
#SayHerName

Plastered on insta,
Again.
It's a woman's work
Standing up
For our sister.
The news that dominates
Framed like women
Should be more careful.
Walk with a friend,
Keys ready to hand,
Cover more skin.
But don't be fearful!
Let's say it with pride.
This isn't a woman's fight.
MEN YOU MUST DO BETTER!
She isn't a belonging,
Not someone's wife,
Daughter or sister.
First
She is a woman,
A person,
No bigger or smaller.
No less or more important.
Her name now etched
Into stone forever.
Another woman's life, stolen.
Sent too early to heaven.
Because society
Refuses to deal

With the truth
And hold accountable
The men
Who simply refuse
To rid themselves
Of ingrained misogyny.
The patriarchy running wild.
Creating a distorted version
of what really happened
And why.
So STAND up men
And be counted.
Sharing a hashtag
Is not going to save us.
So call out your brothers
And stop berating us.
We deserve safety
Not to always feel
Like there ain't none.
How many trending hashtags
Before you rate us?
Treat us like humans
Instead of hurt us?
Give us equal rights
And stop oppressing us?
#MeToo
#ReclaimTheseStreets
And #SayHerName
Have become a trending nature.

It appears almost daily
In an endless battle
Of women standing up
And testifying
The truth of what surrounds us.
We continue to fight
For basic human rights
In the infrastructure of a
Society created to contain us.
We no longer agree
To stay in the lane
Designated for us.
Time to change the story
And report it
In its true nature.
Ring out the names
Of the men
Who kill us!
Because collectively
We feel the pain
Of every woman's cries
When a man decides
He has the power
At his hands
And another one
Of our sisters die.

SAY HER NAME!

#sayhername

Do They Hear You Speak?

Stop!
What you say only has value
If the people you speak it to
Can hear it.
You might breathe your wisdom out,
Kick your feet,
Scream and shout.
But do they really understand?
Do they have the capacity
To see your words with clarity,
Through your written hand?
If you're not preaching to the woke
They will sit and choke
When you need them to stand.
If they are not on your side,
Or their energy reeks of a different vibe,
Surely you can notice your voice
Getting so lost in the unspoken divide.
Do they really hear you?
They might be seeing the same world as you,
But they will never see it from the same view.
Put it into terms
That they can discern
Or you'll be chasing the ghosts
Of your dying verse.
It's not your job to educate them.

Be yourself without explanation.
Hold your head up high
And walk with pride.
If a bee doesn't buzz itself silly
Telling flies to leave shit to live on honey,
Why waste your words away?
Be the GOAT
And row your own boat
In a world that wants carbon copies.

No Response

Hold it all in.
Keep it deep.
For in a minute
There will be no sin.
Drink your drink,
Stare and smile.
Join the laughter
If only for a little while.
Go with the flow.
Soak it all up.
Don't respond
And don't discuss.
Yes and no,
There is no other answer.
Smile sweetly
And barely react.
For you will regret
When the board finally snaps.
Just bite your tongue
And hold tight to your lip.
For in a moment
There will be no sin.

The Hidden

Unless it is your lungs
That breathes the air
That penetrates his body,
That oxygenates his blood
And his brain.
Unless it is your heart
That pumps in aid of his,
Then he is not your body,
He is not your soul
Nor your concern.
He is not your smile
Or your happiness.
He is neither a man nor a woman.
He is a being,
Who breathes as you and I do,
Lingers like a shadow,
Tailgating your human form
And embedding your
Skeleton's mental stability.
He is an object
Neither human nor anatomically alike.
His function is not to live your life.
Yet he interjects
And intercepts
Moments on your timeline.
Reflecting an imitation

Of spot the difference,
Dot to dot
And paint by the missing numbers.
Not colour coordinated
Or linear.
But a chaotic disturbance
And embodiment
Of a life you somewhat choose
And are forced to lead,
Until you realise it is not
He who aids
You to breathe.

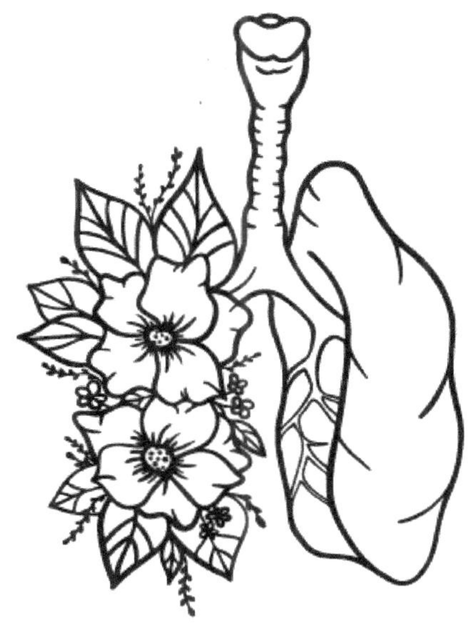

Shhhhhh...

I've got a secret
But no one to tell.
You can't see it.
I'm stuck in its spell.

It's mine, I'm possessive.
I've carried it for so long.
I don't want to share it.
People knowing will surely
Cause things to go wrong.

It's stuck in the dark
But I feel urged to bring it to light.
I'm battling myself
In a constant internal fight.

And so I wear it.
I wear my secret
But cover it up.
I hide it in the light
As a way to keep it in the dark.

I've got control.
It's what I tell myself.
But it devours my soul
So more and more I end up

Losing myself.

You won't see it
Unless you pay attention.
But once you do
You'll notice my
Parallel dimension.

You've seen my secret
All along.
You witnessed my downfall
And played a part in its song.

It's stuck with me.
It will be for life.
Once my demon
My hidden nightly cry.

What once was a secret
Became my teacher
And ultimately
Its release
Became my healer.

A Moment

My hands are trembling,
I can feel them.
I hold them steady
But it's hard work.
I'm hiding the truth
Of my pacing breath
And the pulsating pressure
Vibrating my chest.
My nostrils are flaring
As I avoid your stare.
I'm working hard
To soften my voice,
As I respond to you
Without choice.
Smile on my face
Scoping my escape
From this place.
Seconds ago familiar,
Now an alien space.
My head constantly hopping
From thought to thought.
Oh shit did I lock the door?
A million moments
Within a second in my head.
Inconsistent emotions
Rushing through my veins.

I just want to go to my bed.
My body completely confused
By my response
To a non-threat.
I just don't understand,
What caused this?
Muscles start tensing,
Beads of sweat trickle
From my forehead.
Hair gripping to a
Sticky sweaty neck.
Sorry…
What was it you just said?
Lacking focus,
Trailing thoughts,
In this moment I've become
So
Completely
Lost.

A Split Second

Do you ever just sit
There and think -
What the hell is this?
Head racing,
Thoughts pacing.
My mind feels like
It is stuck in a cameo.
Not knowing
What way to turn.
Is this a lesson to learn?
Questioning my decisions
Before they've been made.
I've almost surrendered,
Feeling like my body
Has been dismembered
From my feeling and thoughts
Again.
My arms feel full
But I've nothing in my hands.
A burden to carry
My shoulders so heavy
But nothing shows
Because visibly
Nothing weighs me down.

Silver Linings

I spun myself a sea of silver linings
Always hunting the best in the worst.
I tore myself apart understanding,
Killing off parts of me with each piece of hurt.

I drowned when the tsunami hit
Flooding my face with the I'm okay mask.
No longer able to swim.
Floating around, feet barely on the ground,
Life overwhelmingly
Feeling more and more dim.

I found a silver lining, but lining it was not
As in the pit of my stomach,
The darkness hadn't forgot.
Retching on the memories of the past,
Finding that my silver had turned into brass.

There is always a silver lining,
It's what they always say.
They will drum to the beat of toxic positivity,
Until they have a bad day.
They say everything happens for a reason
But let's be honest,
Sometimes there is just dismay.

Do You Remember?

Do you remember when you were a teen?
You'd just been flooded with hormones.
Your body never felt the same,
And adults would make comparisons
To peers of the same age.

Do you remember when you were a teen?
When you were constantly told to grow up?
It was like the adult world,
Had completely forgot
That they were once us.

Do you remember when you were a teen?
Your body was non stop changing,
And whilst your hormones were raging
You had adults complaining
Everytime a teenager was seen having fun.

Do you remember being a teen?
Mental health wasn't a mentioned thing.
In this generation, it's a wave of disgrace
The amount of teens without support
Around the pandemic's hidden face.

Do you remember being a teen?
Your bodies were more physically lean.

Generations of increasing obesity,
Technology forever seen.
A generation of children locked in isolation,
Streets an unsafe devastation
And faces constantly attached to a screen.

Do you remember being a teen?
Did you ever feel like adults could see you?
We spend all our time,
Calling a generation a joke.
Pointing out they are addicted to their phones.
But when push comes to shove and we've had
enough,
Why do we just ask them to sit on a computer,
Instead of filling them with love
And filling their tummies with laughter?

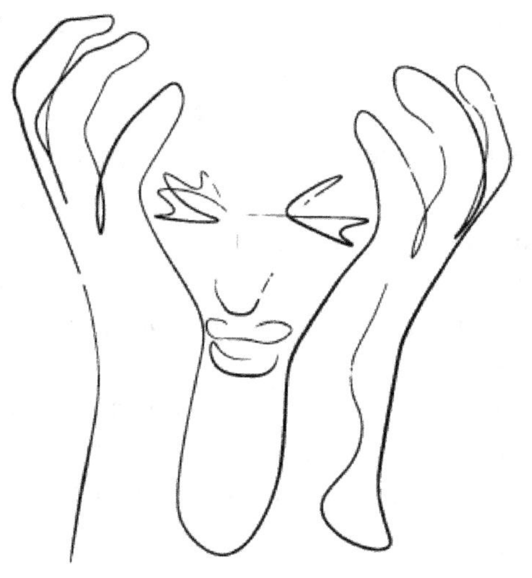

Has Anyone Seen?

It's been a while
And I haven't heard from her.
I'm starting to worry and panic.
Where could she have gone?
It's not usual
For her to be away for so long.
Has anyone seen her?
I wonder if anyone has noticed
That she hasn't been around.
It's been so terribly quiet,
I'll have to keep
My ear to the ground.
What could have happened?
I don't quite understand!
Last time I saw her
She'd been so loud and proud.
Should I put a missing poster out?
What picture could I use?
She might not look the same.
I did over hear someone saying
She just hadn't been herself
But she had no excuse.
Why did no one tell me?
I guess others could see
Something I just couldn't,
Or maybe I saw

But I just didn't want to believe.
Has anyone seen her?
I miss it when she isn't here.
I'm full of sadness
But maybe she just changed.
Perhaps she is hiding from me,
Are we playing a game?
I don't know where she's at,
But surely I should know.
Can someone just please tell me
What is going on?
Oh wait,
I thought I spotted her!
I almost didn't recognise,
Where did it go wrong?
What's this reflection I see?
Is this mirror broken?
Has anyone seen me?

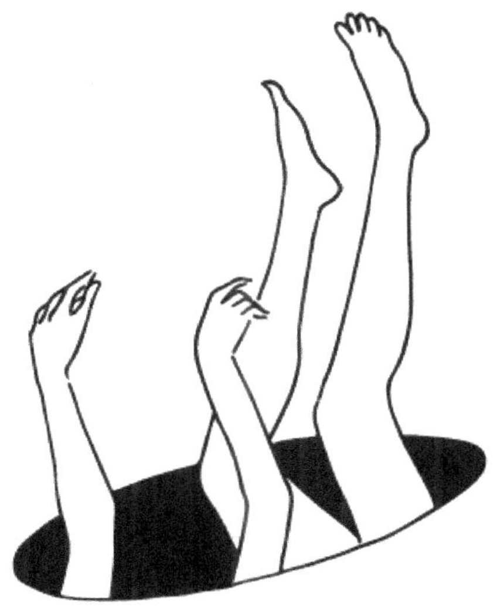

Blue Screen Dream

Don't you think it is simply mad,
That you can be surrounded by people,
Whose only focus is in their hand?
Eyes bulging like a caricature,
No clue where they are going,
Walking into each other.
Eyes on the screen
As they quietly squeak -
Excuse me, and simple pleasantries.

Don't you think it's completely sad,
The things that are lost,
That you can never get back?
For a virtual world and complete enigma,
Stealing your words and your picture.
No longer private,
Information no longer safe,
An online world of people
And bots hiding their faces.

Don't you ever wonder if we will ever get it
back?
Eyes on the real world
Instead of on a screen so flat.
Will children ever live the same
Or forever be attached

To life through a battery pack?
Their only real connection,
Through their phone screen
A stranger's like or comment,
The real blue screen dream.

Can you see technology's impact,
On a dying breed?
Our wars removed from the streets
And taking to the threads,
The internet's call for peace.
We no longer stand up -
Instead in our stories we protest.
One tweet after the other.
Our followers, the new contest.

Can you remember
The time before the storm?
When a blue screen dream
Meant holding our phone no more.
Putting it down without a worry,
Leaving the house with only keys and money.
Our whole life compact on a phone,
It's no wonder why
We live our life in a world without time zones.

Foreign Love

Why is loving yourself so foreign?
When love is all you have to give?
You smile through the
Burning desire to
Simply - fit - in.
You sever your own heart
To heal those of others;
But it warms you like
A night sat by the winter fire.
It keeps your soul burning so
You extend your hand
Leaving your arm at length,
So those who have burned you
Can once again step in.
You take the pain
And turn it into gold,
Using it as an example
Of why you live your life so bold.
With every smile that gets returned
And every moment lived and learned,
You are loving yourself!
Just without it being known.
So keep loving others,
Stay kind and humble.
Burn your fire and break the mould.
Continue to be a soul

To be desired,
Because the platform is already full
Of humans living a life
That is entirely social media wired.

Within Me

I have everything I need
Right here within me.
I hold it all in my smile,
I grasp it in the palm of my hands,
I fold it in my heart.
I see it in the night stars.
It's in every experience.
It's in every moment.
I'll hold and love it,
I'll cherish and grow it.
I have everything I need
Right here within me.

Broken Spine

Sometimes we get stuck
At the end of a chapter.
Our full stop drawn out
Or frozen on a comma.
We struggle to turn the page
Or close the book
And walk away.

We forget to breathe
Or take in the breeze,
Embrace the moment
For exactly what it could be.
Or feel the sun kiss our face,
Our heads are buried in society's rat race.

Simply because we are
Caught up on life's cliffhangers.
Searching for answers
In the what ifs
And could have beens.
Mesmerized by the media we devour.

We forget the control
We really do have.
We wrote our book
And chose our soundtrack.

And like the changing seasons,
Our spine evolves.
No longer the paperback
But a hardback protected with gold.
We have the strength
To change our journey.
Choose our path
And edit our future story.

Why stop at one?
Write a trilogy…
Or more.
You are the encyclopedia
At your very own core.

We often find ourselves
Anchored on,
Pulling us down.
Trapped in the same song,
And replaying the same sounds.

But you've written your past
By your very own hand.
Replace your ink,
Remove your head from the sand.
Blow off the dust
And trust in your seams.

You have the ability
To become empowered.
So keep drawing up your chapters
Hour by hour.
Wisely choose your words,
And your grammar;
For you're the author of your story,
So stand in your power!

Belonging

What is belonging anyway?
Bending over backwards
And reshaping your mould,
To fit someone else in?
Budging over and making room
Losing small but growing pieces of you?

What is fitting in anyway?
Meeting a societal norm
Designed to oppress us!
Being a clone and replicating
That zone -
That fitting in fits in anyway.

What is belonging anyway?
Conforming to the roles bestowed upon you.
Budding your light for others in the room.
Hiding your authenticity for the comfort of
others.
Belonging doesn't sound so cool.

When you let your light shine
And you be your inner you.
The brightness that you radiate
Harmonises with others who are true.
You'll find your people

Who with ease you will be,
Deep in love and comfort
At who you are and want to be.

I Am More

I am more than the tears I cry
When I see myself and don't recognise why.

I am more than the pain I feel
Inflicted by another,
Snapping my achilles heel.

I am more than the trauma I carry
In my bones and in my body.

I am more than the responses I give
When I'm responding with my inner child,
When I'm living as my kid.

I am more than the emotional explosions
When frustration is in motion.

I am more than those really low moments
Because I am strong
And I am healing not broken.

I am more than the strength you see
For I am leading the way for me.

I am more than the period you are blaming.

I am more than the gender I am claiming.

I am more than the job I am holding.

I am more than the wallet I am folding.

I am more than everything you see.

Because inside there is so much more to me.

Unconditional Love

I could feel it growing,
This smile on my face.
From resting b face
To a face full of cheerful grace.

I could feel it warming,
This feeling in my chest
My heart filling up with
The warmth of the
Beating in my chest.

I could feel it overwhelmingly,
Filling up my eyes.
Slowly welling up
As happy tears dripped
From my eyes.

I could feel it so clearly,
As my mind slowed its pace.
Just sat in happy thought,
Enjoying the moment's embrace.

I could feel it in my body,
Shoulders no longer hunched up
But slowly they relaxed
As I realised I felt so fully

An unconditional love.

I could feel it so joyfully,
As his little paws reached up
Wagging his tail
In his joyful exhale
Of seeing his Mum.

Seeds

57

Take a moment.
Breathe.
Look back and see the trampled path,
The start you can no longer see.
Do you realise how far
You really have come?
From seed to root to tree.
Your flowers are blossoming,
Your leaves will fall.
But with each season
And change
They will respawn.
Your path grows longer with age.
You've got this!
It's rooted in your veins.
Stand in your power
Through all the storms
And changing weather;
A new path you will sow.
With every seed that you plant
And every root they sprout,
Love and kindness will flow.
Inside you
Is the truth and love you need,
It is the water you need to reap your seeds.
So stop!

Take a minute.
Breathe.
Look back at the path that you have walked.
The start and middle you can no longer see.
Its seeds have blossomed
And buzz with bees.
As you look - you will see
The answer was always you.
You are all you need!

You Are

Genuine is genuine.
Passionate is passionate.
Tough is tough.
Intelligent is intelligent.
Beautiful is beautiful.
Courageous is courageous.
Brave is brave.
Kind is kind.
Considerate is considerate.
Hilarious is hilarious.
Warm-hearted is warm-hearted.
Reliable is reliable.
Sincere is sincere.
Adventurous is adventurous.
Pretty is pretty.
Amazing is amazing.
Powerful is powerful.
Strong is strong.
Emotional is emotional.
Grateful is grateful.
Worthy is worthy.
You are you.

Now read it again and change the last word of
each sentence to you.

That is what you are, and you can be them all at once.

Never forget these words, you are worth not just one, but all of them and so many more.

www.ingramcontent.com/pod-product-compliance
Lightning Source LLC
Chambersburg PA
CBHW070554160726
48003CB00005B/2043